THE MYSTERY OF
THE SPHINX

by Karen Latchana Kenney

Content Consultant
Devin Stewart
Arabic and Islamic Studies
Emory University

Core Library

An Imprint of Abdo Publishing
abdopublishing.com

abdopublishing.com

Published by Abdo Publishing, a division of ABDO, PO Box 398166, Minneapolis, Minnesota 55439. Copyright © 2016 by Abdo Consulting Group, Inc. International copyrights reserved in all countries. No part of this book may be reproduced in any form without written permission from the publisher. Core Library™ is a trademark and logo of Abdo Publishing.

Printed in the United States of America, North Mankato, Minnesota
092015
012016

Cover Photo: Shutterstock Images
Interior Photos: Shutterstock Images, 1, 18, 45; iStockphoto, 4, 24, 30, 43; C. H. Graves/Library of Congress, 7; Felice A. Beato, 10; Kyodo/AP Images, 13; Dorling Kindersley/Thinkstock, 15, 23; Nestor Noci/Shutterstock Images, 27; Khaled Elfiqi/EPA/Newscom, 36; Amr Nabil/AP Images, 40

Editor: Mirella Miller
Series Designer: Ryan Gale

Library of Congress Control Number: 2015945994

Cataloging-in-Publication Data
Kenney, Karen Latchana.
 The mystery of the Sphinx / Karen Latchana Kenney.
  p. cm. -- (Mysteries of history)
ISBN 978-1-68078-027-7 (lib. bdg.)
Includes bibliographical references and index.
1. Sphinxes (Mythology)--Juvenile literature. 2. Great Sphinx (Egypt)--Juvenile literature.   I. Title.
398.24--dc23

                                                        2015945994

CONTENTS

CHAPTER ONE

SECRETS OF THE SPHINX

T he sands of the Sahara Desert hold many secrets of civilizations past. In Egypt, sand almost buried an ancient wonder: the Great Sphinx of Giza, a giant statue with the face of a king and the body of a lion. The Sphinx stands guard over three great pyramids on the outskirts of Cairo, Egypt, in an area known as the Giza Plateau. The Sphinx and the pyramids have survived thousands of

The Great Sphinx on the Giza Plateau has been surrounded by questions since its discovery.

The Sphinx's Name

The original name of the Sphinx is unknown. Later generations of Egyptians called it Hor-em-akhet, which translates in English to "Horus in the Horizon." It was likely named the Great Sphinx approximately 2,000 years after it was built. The word *sphinx* comes from ancient Greece. It was part of Greek mythology, used for a creature with a lion's body and woman's head. The sphinx of Greek mythology was known to be a riddler. A sphinx became a symbol of hidden meaning.

years. But several times the body of the Sphinx has been found buried in sand. Mystery surrounds this sculpture, and many questions about it remain unanswered. Why was it built? How old is it? And is anything hidden deep inside?

For centuries only the Sphinx's head could be seen. Blowing desert sands had buried the sculpture's body. Still, kings, emperors, explorers, and tourists traveled to see the ancient wonder. Some carved messages on the Sphinx. One ancient Greek message suggests gods made the Sphinx. Medieval Arab scholars called the Sphinx the

A group of people, along with their donkeys and camels, gather in front of the Sphinx in the early 1900s.

"Father of Terror." Some believed it protected the land and crops nearby. Later tourists sat on camels beside it or even stood on the Sphinx itself, posing for photographs. It took major excavations to reveal the full Sphinx.

The head and body of the Sphinx remain above ground today, showing its incredible length of 240 feet (73 m). From its outstretched front paws to its curled tail, it is slightly shorter than a football field. The full height to the top of the Sphinx's head is 66 feet (20 m).

Saving the Sphinx

Over many years, the Sphinx's body wore away. Different cultures placed huge limestone blocks around the body. They wanted to protect the Sphinx's form. The limestone blocks came from a nearby quarry and were used to build other structures on the plateau, such as the temples. The Great Sphinx is made of one piece of stone. Masons carved the gigantic sculpture from the middle section of the quarry.

The three pyramids behind the Sphinx were marked for the pharaohs who had them built. These large monuments were symbols of the pharaohs' power. They were giant tombs that held things the pharaohs believed they would need in the afterlife. The pharaohs thought they would become gods after they died.

The Great Sphinx's builders left no markings. Its form does not fit ancient Egyptian images of gods either. Egyptian gods and goddesses had animal heads and human bodies. But the Sphinx is different. It has a human head and a lion's body.

Nothing was written about the Great Sphinx on the tombs in the Giza Plateau. Throughout the centuries, scholars and scientists have studied the Sphinx. Many have worked to preserve its form, which has slowly worn down in the desert conditions. Many still wonder about its purpose. Why was the Great Sphinx built? And what secrets does this monumental sculpture hold?

PERSPECTIVES
Arab Beliefs

Medieval Arab scholars and explorers wondered why the Great Sphinx existed. Many accounts suggest the sculpture was connected to the stars. Al-Idrisi, an Arab geographer from the 1100s, wrote of the Sphinx's alignment with the sun. The rising sun shone between the Sphinx's eyes. Another Arab theory was that the Sphinx reversed a person's fortune. With one look at the Sphinx, a rich man would become poor. If a person lacked certain abilities, he could gain them by looking at the sculpture.

CHAPTER TWO

UNCOVERING A GIANT

Pharaohs and other ancient Egyptians once worshipped the Great Sphinx. They repaired its eroding body. The ancient Romans would later do the same. Then time forgot the Great Sphinx. It became a giant stone head sticking out of the desert sands. Modern explorers thought there must be more to the sculpture. They worked to free the body

At different points throughout history, only the Sphinx's head was visible above the sand.

beneath. Would it tell them more about the Sphinx's history and purpose?

Modern archaeologists made attempts to clear the sand from the body of the Sphinx. Italian explorer Giovanni Caviglia tried in 1816 and 1817. He led a team of 100 workers who uncovered the breast and front paws of the Sphinx. Caviglia also found parts of a beard and a headdress. Between its paws stood a flat stone almost 12 feet (3.7 m) tall, covered with ancient Egyptian writing. The stone slab, called the Dream Stela, was made during the reign of the Egyptian pharaoh Thutmose IV. Caviglia also discovered a Roman addition to the site. It was a staircase that led to the floor of the temple in front of the Sphinx. Caviglia's workers dug 65 feet (20 m) deep in search of more clues. But sand slides stopped the excavation.

Mid- to Late 1800s

British officer Richard Howard-Vyse tried to uncover the Sphinx in the 1830s. He drilled into

Egypt's Antiquities Minister Mamdouh el-Damaty points to the Dream Stela between the Sphinx's paws.

the Sphinx's body with metal rods. He was looking for markings made by its builders. The rods broke and Howard-Vyse's team tried to remove them with gunpowder explosions. It did not work. Luckily no major harm was done to the Sphinx.

The Sphinx was cleared again several times between the 1840s and 1880s. But the sands crept back to cover the Sphinx again. Between the 1920s and 1930s, excavations finally uncovered the entire Sphinx.

The Missing Nose

Much of the Sphinx is still visible. But one very noticeable facial feature is missing—its nose. It does not seem likely that it fell off. One theory is that the nose was destroyed in 1378. A Sufi Muslim, Muhammad Sa'im al-Dahr, was angry that Egyptians were praying to the Sphinx. He may have destroyed the nose in an effort to stop the people's reverence of the sculpture. This is only a theory. No one knows how the Sphinx lost its nose.

Studying the Sphinx

After the final excavation of the Sphinx and pyramids, scientists were able to study the Giza Plateau structures. They saw that the Sphinx was one of many structures on the Giza Plateau. The structures were connected and seemed to be part of a complex. Scientists also uncovered the restorations made by the ancient Egyptians and the Romans.

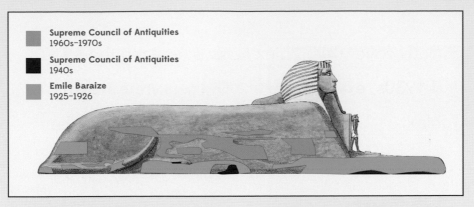

Ancient Repairs

Explorers who found the Great Sphinx also restored it. They wanted to preserve the ancient sculpture for future generations. Traces of their preservation work remain today. This map shows where stone blocks were added to the Sphinx's body. Do you think these repairs helped the Sphinx? What might have happened to the sculpture if ancient cultures had not added stone blocks?

One of the excavators in the early 1900s, Emile Baraize of France, repaired parts of the Sphinx with concrete. After Baraize's restoration work, the Egyptian Antiquities Organization, later called the Supreme Council of Antiquities (SCA), took over. The SCA continues to protect and restore the Sphinx.

Scientists and scholars still study the Sphinx. Clues tell them what the Sphinx may have looked like when it was built. The Sphinx was likely brightly painted in ancient times. A hole in its head might have held a headdress. The sculpture may have also had a beard. There were abandoned tools and stone blocks found. This and other evidence show the Sphinx was left unfinished. No one knows why.

After some restoration, scientists had more clues to the Sphinx's purpose. They could begin to construct their theories. The Sphinx was finally fully visible, but many questions remained unanswered.

Giovanni Battista Caviglia excavated part of the Great Sphinx in 1817. He found a Greek inscription on the sculpture's left paw. It speaks of the Sphinx and its place on the plateau. It also mentions the Greek gods and goddesses of Latona, Vulcan, and Pallas:

Thy form stupendous here the gods have placed,
Sparing each spot of harvest-bearing land;
And with this mighty work of art have graced,
A rocky isle encumbered once with sand;
Not that fierce Sphinx that Thebes erewhile laid waste,
But great Latona's servant, mild and bland;
Watching that prince beloved, who fills the throne
Of Egypt's plains, and calls the Nile his own.
That heavenly monarch, who his foes defies:
Like Vulcan powerful, and like Pallas wise.

Source: Gustaf Clemens Hebbe. History of the World. *New York: DeWitt and Davenport, 1848. Print. 232.*

What's the Big Idea?
Read this passage closely. What do you think the author was saying about the Great Sphinx? Write your opinion based upon this source. Use two to three examples from the source to back up your opinion.

CHAPTER THREE

THE SPHINX'S AGE

Behind the Sphinx are three pyramids, built for the powerful pharaohs Khafre, Khufu, and Menkaure. The pharaohs were seen as divine rulers. When they died, the pharaohs believed they would become gods. Their great pyramids sent them into the afterlife.

Buried in sand, the pyramids, temples, and Sphinx seemed to be separate. After uncovering much of the

Egyptians believed pharaohs could speak with the gods.

Giza Plateau, scholars saw the temples linked to the three pyramids by causeways. The buildings aligned to each other and the sun's path across the sky. It gave scholars clues to the origins of the Sphinx. The Sphinx seemed to align with Khafre's pyramid. But others disagree. Some believe the Sphinx is much older than the pyramid. Without any markings, the true age of the Sphinx is unknown. When was it really built? And which pharaoh was it built for?

Khafre's Sphinx

Many scholars believe the Sphinx was built around 2500 BCE for Khafre. He ruled Egypt from 2520 to 2494 BCE. The Sphinx may have been built while Khafre was still alive.

Part of the quarry around the Sphinx aligns with the Pyramid of Khafre's causeway. A drainage channel from the causeway empties into the quarry. Why would workers allow water to flow toward the Sphinx? Some believe this means the Sphinx was built after the causeway.

Khafre's temple sits at the end of the causeway. Right next to it is the Sphinx Temple. Temples were usually built after a pharaoh's death. Both temples' stones seem to have been cut from the quarry around the Sphinx. This may mean the Sphinx Temple and the Sphinx were built at the same time.

Some scholars believe the Sphinx was built for Khafre's father, Khufu. Khufu's pyramid, built in 2550 BCE, is north of the Sphinx. But Khafre's causeway does not head east, as most do. This angle may mean the Sphinx already

PERSPECTIVES
Proof of Its Age?

Egyptian archeologist Zahi Hawass headed the SCA and also directed excavations on the Giza Plateau. He has made many discoveries there too. Hawass believes the Sphinx cannot date to 7000 to 5000 BCE. If a civilization existed then, the people would have left artifacts. Hawass states the oldest artifacts in Egypt date to 5,000 years ago. He believes this proves the Sphinx could not have been built at an earlier date.

existed to the pyramid's east. The causeway was then built around the Sphinx.

Another clue to its age lies in the Sphinx's face. Many believe it is either Khafre or Khufu's face. The only known true image of Khufu is on a sculpture at the Egyptian Museum in Cairo, Egypt. The small sculpture has a broad face and deeply set eyes. It does not have a beard. In every image of Khafre, the pharaoh has a beard. Some think the Sphinx's face is a better match to Khufu. This would mean the Sphinx was built before Khafre's rule.

A Much Older Sphinx

Another theory sets the Sphinx much further back in time. This theory follows the climate conditions of the Giza Plateau. It looks at the erosion on the Sphinx's body. While its head has survived fairly well, the Sphinx's body has not. French mathematician R. A. Schwaller de Lubicz believed water, not winds and sand, eroded the body. Yet the amount of water needed to erode the Sphinx had not fallen

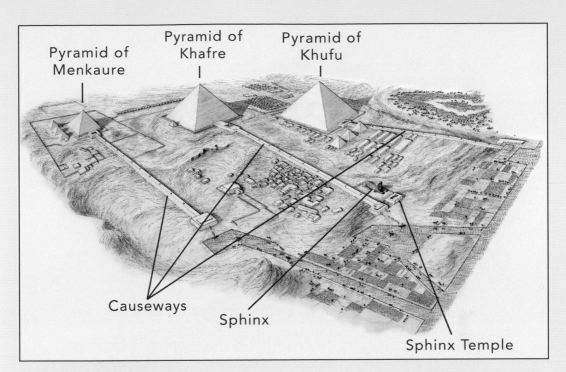

The Giza Plateau

This map shows the structures on the Giza Plateau. Some of its structures connect to one another by long causeways. The area by the Sphinx connects with the Pyramid of Khafre. Does the map help you understand how the Sphinx might have been built at the same time as Khafre's pyramid?

in Egypt in thousands of years. If water eroded the Sphinx, the sculpture could date back to between 7000 and 5000 BCE. So far there is no evidence Egyptians existed in the area at that time. Some guess an advanced civilization existed then. They may have built the Sphinx. The question remains: How old is the Sphinx?

CHAPTER FOUR

GUARDIAN OF THE HORIZON

The Sphinx has the head of a human and the body of a lion. Its form and position may give clues to its purpose. Was it meant to be the symbol of a sun god? The sun was a powerful force in ancient Egyptian religion. The Sphinx faces east, where the sun rises. Is it guarding the horizon?

Ancient Egyptians considered the lion a symbol of a powerful guardian. Egyptian writing often compares

Some researchers wonder if the Sphinx was built to guard the horizon.

A Cosmic Engine?

American archaeologist Mark Lehner believes the Sphinx was made as a kind of cosmic engine. It seems to capture and use the power of the sun. Lehner and other Egyptologists have noticed different connections to the sun at the site. The Sphinx Temple has 24 pillars, perhaps for each hour of a day. Lehner noticed that the sun sets over the Sphinx's shoulder. It also sets on the south side of Khafre's pyramid. The sun looks like it connects the two structures. Lehner believes the Sphinx could have been made as an offering to the sun from Khafre. As it moved across the sky, the sun could send Khafre's soul from Earth to the afterlife.

pharaohs to lions. Images often show pharaohs as lions. Yet a lion is wild and did not have the wisdom of a pharaoh. Placing a pharaoh's head on a lion's body created a creature both fierce and wise.

The Dream Stela

A link between the Sphinx and the god Horus appears on the large stone slab found between the Sphinx's front paws in 1817. Horus was a god whose eyes represented the sun and moon. He was the son of the sun god, Ra. Thutmose IV, the pharaoh of Egypt

Horus was often pictured as a falcon or as a man with a falcon head.

from 1400 to 1390 BCE, left the Dream Stela there. That may have been more than 1,000 years after the Sphinx was made.

The slab describes a dream Thutmose IV had before he was a pharaoh. In the dream, Horus appeared as the Sphinx and spoke to Thutmose IV. Horus promised to make Thutmose IV pharaoh if he was freed from the sand. Thutmose IV cleared the sand from the Sphinx, became pharaoh, and created

The Power of a Dream

Horus appeared as the Sphinx in Thutmose IV's dream. The future pharaoh was on the plateau one hot day and took shelter in the shade of the Sphinx. He fell asleep and had the dream. In ancient Egypt, dreams were believed to have meaning. It was unusual for gods to speak to humans. But ancient Egyptians believed gods spoke to pharaohs. This record of the dream likely gave Thutmose IV a powerful claim to the throne. Only a future pharaoh could receive such a message from Horus.

the Dream Stela between the Sphinx's paws. The dream may or may not have been real. But it became an important moment in the Sphinx's history.

Cult of the Sphinx

The Sphinx was restored and became a center of religious activity in Egypt between 1550 and 1070 BCE. The Sphinx became known as Hor-em-akhet. This name means "Horus in the horizon." A chapel was built between the Sphinx's front paws. New pharaohs came to the chapel at the beginning of their rule. They made offerings to the Sphinx. They may have believed the Sphinx made the pharaohs true rulers of Egypt. The pharaohs left records of their visits. They also built monuments to the Sphinx. People made pilgrimages to see the Sphinx and left small statues at the site. But this worship of the Sphinx as a god only seems to have appeared during the period of Egyptian history known as the New Kingdom, between approximately 1550 and 1070 BCE. How did Egyptians view the Sphinx in the centuries before? Was it created for the same purpose?

FURTHER EVIDENCE

Chapter Four covers the theory that the Sphinx represented a sun god. It also discusses the stone tablet found between the Sphinx's paws. What was one of the main points of this chapter? What evidence is included to support this point? Read the interview at the website below. Does the information on the website support the main point of the chapter? Does it present new evidence?

The Dream Stela
mycorelibrary.com/sphinx

CHAPTER FIVE

THE HIDDEN CHAMBER THEORY

Discovering hidden rooms in Egyptian structures is not unusual. Tunnels and chambers have been found in the three Giza pyramids. Some believe there are more to be found inside the Sphinx. Most Egyptologists do not support this idea. But some drawings show the Great Sphinx differently than the Sphinx as it is seen today. It rests on a base. Sometimes the base has a door. It has led

Archaeologists continue to find hidden rooms among the Giza pyramids.

some to wonder if a hidden chamber exists inside the Sphinx.

Lost Hall of Records

One theory of a hidden chamber came from Edgar Cayce. He was an American born in 1877 who claimed to be psychic. He believed he could predict future events while in a sleeplike trance. In his trances, Cayce predicted that a hall of records would be found under the Sphinx. He told of refugees from the mythical sunken city of Atlantis who buried their secrets in a chamber there.

Despite having no proof, many people believed Cayce's theory. Cayce founded the Association for Research and Enlightenment (ARE) in 1931. ARE funded expeditions to search the Giza Plateau. Two American women raised funds to conduct an independent search of the Sphinx in 1957. Egyptian officials gave them permission to drill holes into the base of the Sphinx. The women thought the builders might have left information about a hidden chamber beneath limestone blocks by the paws. The women inspired others to explore the Sphinx further.

Seismic Study

In the early 1990s, a new study reported to have found something. John Anthony West was an amateur Egyptologist. He supported the idea that rain had weathered the Sphinx. West organized a scientific team to study the Sphinx. This team included geophysicist Dr. Thomas Dobecki. At the Sphinx site, Dobecki used special equipment that studies seismic vibrations.

What Dobecki found was unusual. His results indicated the bedrock below the paws contained cavities. He also found cavities along the sides of

PERSPECTIVES
Stanford Research Institute Findings

In 1977 and 1978, one of the biggest searches was done at the Sphinx. Part of its funds came from ARE. The Stanford Research Institute used new technology to try to find a chamber. It sent electrical pulses through the Sphinx to find empty spaces in the rock. The results only showed small channels for groundwater and other small holes. No large chambers were seen.

The Legend of Atlantis

The ancient Greek philosopher Plato wrote about the lost civilization of Atlantis. Atlantis was once a city of advanced people. Their city consisted of linked islands filled with great riches, such as gold and silver. Their civilization lived 9,000 years before Plato's time. But the people of Atlantis became greedy and immoral. The gods wanted to punish them. Fire erupted and earthquakes shook the land. As the legend tells, the city and its civilization sank to the bottom of the sea.

the Sphinx. One cavity did not seem to be a natural shape. Dobecki thought it must have been manmade. The results supported Cayce's prediction.

Before the team could find more information, they were stopped. Zahi Hawass, who was then the head of the Supreme Council of Antiquities, accused them of tampering with the Sphinx. The team had to leave the site. They believed they had found something. But they would never know exactly what their instruments detected. Was it truly a hidden chamber?

In one of Cayce's psychic readings, he described the entrance to the Sphinx's secret chamber. He said:

> *There is a chamber or passage from the right forepaw to this entrance of the record chamber or record tomb. This position lies, as the sun rises from the waters, the line of shadow or light falls between the paws of the Sphinx, that was later set as the sentinel or guard . . .*

Source: Robert Bauval. Secret Chamber Revisited: The Quest for the Lost Knowledge of Ancient Egypt. *Toronto: Bear & Company, 2014. Print. 245.*

Changing Minds

The writer discusses what the entrance of the Sphinx's secret chamber looks like. What does he say that leads you to believe this chamber is real? Read back through the chapter for other clues. Do you believe there is a secret chamber? Why or why not?

CHAPTER SIX

FUTURE OF THE SPHINX

Many questions remain about what might be inside the Sphinx. But something alarming is happening on the outside of the Sphinx. The Egyptian government wants to do all it can to preserve the sculpture for future generations. The problem is how to do that safely.

Some repairs done in the 1920s and 1980s did more damage than good. Cement and gypsum mortar

Some restorations on the Sphinx have caused damage to the statue.

Revolution and the Sphinx

In 2011 a revolution erupted in Cairo. It forced the Egyptian president out of power, and the military took control. Tourism to the country decreased dramatically. Without tourism, funds for restoring the structures on the Giza Plateau have dropped. The new government also forced Hawass from his role in the Supreme Council of Antiquities. Many antiquities projects have been stalled. Officials have made mistakes in managing the ancient monuments. Some worry about the future of the ancient structures on the Giza Plateau and around the country.

used to make repairs actually caused more cracks in the statue's limestone. In the 1990s, the cement and mortar were removed. Better repairs were made. But in the 2000s, large flakes of limestone began falling off the Sphinx. Sewage dumped in a nearby canal was blamed. The moisture dissolves salt in the rock, making it crumble off in pieces. Today the large city of Cairo borders the ancient structures on the Giza Plateau. Pollution from the city also threatens the Sphinx.

And some militant Islamic groups have declared that the Sphinx should be destroyed. They say it is a pagan idol that goes against their religious beliefs.

The Supreme Council of Antiquities is in charge of preserving the sculpture. It also decides who can study the Sphinx. Government officials have said they are open to further research on the plateau but will only grant access to teams that come from well-known academic institutions.

PERSPECTIVES
Blocking Research?

Without Hawass monitoring, some scholars worry ancient Egyptian structures may suffer. But John Anthony West believes Hawass blocked important research. Hawass has become a superstar of everything related to ancient Egypt. Hawass sometimes challenged the theories of Western scholars and others, questioning whether their theories were credible and convincing. Most Egyptologists agree with Hawass's work. He was the keeper of all Egyptian monuments, and he kept tight control. For amateur theorists, however, the removal of Hawass may mean the opening of Egypt's monuments for further research.

With more research and work, researchers such as Hawass uncovered more answers in the mystery of the Sphinx.

Will people ever know how old the Great Sphinx is? Or will scholars ever find out why it was made? These mysteries might not be solved. The Great Sphinx may always keep its biggest secrets concealed.

EXPLORE ONLINE

Chapter Six discusses threats to the Sphinx. The article at the website below goes into more depth on this topic. Does the article answer any of the questions you had about the problems facing the Great Sphinx?

Saving the Sphinx
mycorelibrary.com/sphinx

The Sphinx was built during Khafre's rule.

Evidence for:

- The Sphinx quarry aligns with the causeway to Khafre's pyramid.

Evidence against:

- The Sphinx Temple stones were cut from the same stones as Khafre's temple. This may mean they were built at the same time after Khafre's death.

The Sphinx was built during Khufu's rule.

Evidence for:

- The Sphinx may be an image of Khufu.

Evidence against:

- Giovanni Caviglia thought he found part of a beard during his excavation. If the Sphinx had a beard, it was likely made for Khafre.

The weathering on the Sphinx means it is older than the pyramids.

Evidence for:

- The amount of water needed to erode the Sphinx has not fallen in Egypt in thousands of years.

Evidence against:

- The geology of the rock explains why the body has eroded so much. The body's rock is much softer than the lower layer and the head.

Tell the Tale

Chapter Two describes Giovanni Caviglia's excavation of the Great Sphinx. Imagine you were part of his team of explorers. Describe what it was like to find the large stone slab between the Sphinx's paws. Write 200 words about the experience. Was it a surprising find?

Surprise Me

Chapter Five describes an unusual theory about the Sphinx. It suggests there is a hidden chamber inside. After reading this book, what two or three ideas or facts did you find most surprising? Write a few sentences about each idea or fact. Why did you find each idea or fact surprising?

Dig Deeper

After reading this book, what questions do you still have about the purpose of the Great Sphinx? With an adult's help, find a few reliable sources that can help you answer your questions. Write a paragraph about what you learned.

Say What?

Studying ancient Egypt and the Great Sphinx can mean learning a lot of new vocabulary. Find five words in this book you've never heard before. Use a dictionary to find out what they mean. Then write the meanings in your own words, and use each word in a sentence.

GLOSSARY

archaeologists
scientists that study bones and tools of ancient people to learn about their lives and activities

causeways
raised roads that go over water or wet ground

cavities
hollow spaces inside something

civilization
a highly developed society

Egyptologists
people who study ancient Egyptian language and culture

excavation
to dig in the ground to find remains

headdress
a decorated covering for the head

mythology
the traditional stories or beliefs of a culture or society

pharaoh
the title used for kings of ancient Egypt

preservation
protecting something so that it stays in its original form

quarry
a place where stone is dug up from the ground

restoration
bringing something back to an original or better condition

LEARN MORE

Books

Arlon, Penelope. *Ancient Egypt*. New York: Scholastic, 2014.

Henzel, Cynthia Kennedy. *Pyramids of Egypt*. Minneapolis, MN: Abdo, 2011.

The Mysteries of Egypt's Pyramids: The Secrets of the Pharaoh. Chicago: World Book, 2015.

Websites

To learn more about Mysteries of History, visit **booklinks.abdopublishing.com**. These links are routinely monitored and updated to provide the most current information available.

Visit **mycorelibrary.com** for free additional tools for teachers and students.

INDEX

ABOUT THE AUTHOR

Karen Latchana Kenney is a Minnesota author and editor who has written more than 100 books for kids. Kenney loves to research the many mysteries of our world.